Retreat: A Way Forward

poems by

Harry Moore

Finishing Line Press
Georgetown, Kentucky

Retreat: A Way Forward

*Dedicated to my talented and generous companions
Abel, Cody, Debra, Julie, and Rachel*

*With genuine thanks to Jentel Artist Residency:
Neltje, Mary Jane, Melissa, and
Suburban driver par excellence, Lynn*

To Poets & Writers, especially Bonnie, Lynne, and Elliott

To Maureen Egen for her generosity

*And with special thanks to Bill
for his keen eye and unfailing support.*

Copyright © 2017 by Harry Moore
ISBN 978-1-63534-305-2 First Edition
All rights reserved under International and Pan-American Copyright Conventions.
No part of this book may be reproduced in any manner whatsoever without written permission from the publisher, except in the case of brief quotations embodied in critical articles and reviews.

ACKNOWLEDGMENTS

My thanks to the following periodicals, in which poems in this collection first appeared.

The Penwood Review ~ "If God Were gravity."
Ship of Fools ~ "Eros."

Publisher: Leah Maines

Editor: Christen Kincaid

Cover Art: Julie Wills

Author Photo: Harry Moore

Cover Design: Elizabeth Maines McCleavy

Printed in the USA on acid-free paper.
Order online: www.finishinglinepress.com
　　　　　also available on amazon.com

Author inquiries and mail orders:
Finishing Line Press
P. O. Box 1626
Georgetown, Kentucky 40324
U. S. A.

Table of Contents

Retreat 1
Creekside Muse 2
Week One 4
The Collector 5
Letting Go 6
The Geologist and the Poet at the Art Reception 7
Week Two: Lunar Eclipse 9
Old Journals 10
Summer of Discontent 11
Turning Away 12
Eros 13
Forbidding Mourning 14
Week Three 15
Sunrise, Sunset 16
A Small Voice 17
Deus Absconditis 20
Prayer (I) 21
Sacred Space 22
If God Were Gravity 24
Week Four: Winding Down at the Occidental 25
The Valley of Shadow 27
Prayer (II) 28
Fear No Evil 30
Departure 31
Legacy 33

"And if you're lost enough to find yourself
By now, pull in your ladder road behind you
. . . .
Then make yourself at home."
(Robert Frost, "Directive")

Retreat

He knew the long journey out would be
also a journey in, three days alone in a
car, across eight states, a retreat,
drawing back into decades of old
journals packed behind him in dusty
briefcases with rusty snaps and hinges,
in a whiskey box coming apart—fits
and starts, zigzag, a course he may
or may not be able to see from some
foothill he climbs.

                     Some versions of himself
are dead, he's sure, like the prophet he became
at thirteen, declaiming truth to a reluctant world.
But the restless romantic pacing inside every
house that hems him in may not be so strange,
nor the tortured pilgrim who wakes in panic that
he's lost his way. His vaunted contentment with
mystery may or may not smooth his sleep.

Di-vorce, a turning aside or away, occurred
long before he moved out, and he hardly
dares hear again the tearing of flesh as he
pulled away from his children. Are those
nerves numb, scarred over, and what damage
to a battered conscience? Dare he enter
again—after building for decades the bright
life he escaped to—the moral jungle he
hacked at for two years, every road blocked
by a dark tangle till he ran in circles weeping?

In the new haven he arrives at, open
to a broad sky, he roams like the wanderer
he will always be, eager for magpies, wild
turkeys, meadowlarks, porcupines, deer
grazing in alfalfa fields, and in the rising
foothills across the creek, a medley of parched
and twisted grasses, weeds, shrubs, and trees
he's yet to name.

Creekside Muse

Whole prairies from his Deep South home,
he sits at a rough-hewn table—his altar—
facing east in the Sunrise Studio, the robust

current of Piney Creek audible through
the cracked window. It is an arranged
marriage, an exotic affair his family

and his whole world watch and approve of.
But will she come, brushing his arm as she
kneels beside him, hair disheveled and

smelling of morning air? Is she in the wind-
shaken leaves of aspen, with the prairie
rattlers he watches for on rocky foothill

hikes, in the names of box elder, potentilla,
cottonwood that he repeats like a litany?
He writes letters, e-mails, calls home in case

he left her there. Maybe she's the tall dark
one from Marfa who runs every morning.
He hopes she didn't go down in carnage

on the long drive—tufts of white fur clinging
to flattened rabbit pelts, dead raccoons, skunks,
badgers, a coyote's contorted carcass, gutted

deer pecked at by crows and magpies. How will
he know it's her and not a soaring redtail,
a wren hopping by the door, antelope fleeing

cannon booms in alfalfa fields? If he seems
not to care, reads fiction, old journals, theology,
will that draw her; does she disdain easy?

If he chats with other guests about wood
and stone, their children, teaching, will she
think him worthy? When he wakes at 2:00 a.m.

will she whisper things he must write till dawn?
And when he sits before the rising sun while the creek
bears the hours away, will she kneel beside him?

Week One

They move like monks about the grounds,
past cottonwood, spruce, late-blooming

cinquefoil, eyes cast down as if in holy
reverie, coming up to nod, speak, move on.

They work in secret studios or slip quietly
across the bridge to walk the hallowed

thousand acres, stony foothills and gulches,
meeting at mealtime for guarded talk

about work, over soups, salads of their
own making, after-dinner levity absorbed

into the ritual, movies upstairs they may
or may not stay awake for before retiring

to their solitary cells. Their movements are
a mantra, half-stunned and incredulous

at all they've walked away from, supplication
to all gods for some kindness, some lasting form

snatched from the creek's relentless current.

The Collector

Diving into the lake, he found
scraps of childhood poems, birthday
jingles reeking of Hallmark, effusions
on trees, mountains, and summer rain,
fruit of too much time with Wordsworth,
one short story from high school about
disappointment, high-minded lamentations
at the age's moral laxity, anguished
confessions of his own failings, enough
ink about God to paint a village with,
analyses of all problems into their
several parts, as if this was the dance
he knew and walking was too easy,
no comment on public affairs, repeated
self-assessment, like marking a child's
height on the door jamb to chart his growth,
a wicked self-irony wielded like a whip,
memos and letters from work that he
thought incisive, witty, or smartly phrased,
and scattered throughout, like crumbs
beside a winding trail, the names
of all the girls he ever fancied.

Letting Go

The worm bursts its cocoon, snakes
shed old skin, trees drop their leaves
for next year's buds. But I hold on,

like a junkyard piled with rusted cars,
tractors, horse-drawn hay rakes. Not for
parts or the price of scrap, but for

feelings that fade under a blistering sun,
leach into the soil. I keep buckets—whole
cisterns brimming with last year's storm.

The Geologist and the Poet at the Art Reception

In tan vest and jeans, he could be my
doppelganger but for the white hair.
A geologist, he says, veteran with coal
and now oil and natural gas. His wife
is on the Foundation Board, hence this
swimming in an artsy sea. Around us
are exhibited the soils, weeds, trees,
hills, creeks, and native costumes of
the valley, art celebrating place.

We need a balance, he says, between
consumption and beauty, extraction
and restoration, something bureaucrats
bungle and schools do not teach. I agree—
bred to the farm, then handed a pen; surely
we can live and keep the landscape.

***

Who knows, I wonder, what secrets
lie beneath the placid surface around
us—why the young woman sipping merlot
has her ankles crossed, if the man with
the piled plate is poor or just hungry,
how much the desire for fame—Milton's
last infirmity of a noble mind—infects
the art objects lining the wall.

                                             I think
of journals back in my studio—fifty years
of scribbling ripe with poetic possibility—
nuggets to be mined, scenes shaped, refined,
recast for effect. What to make of this digging?
Do I see with Hawthorne's icy eyes, boring in,
blasting, dragging long-buried hurt to the light—
careless of others glad enough to leave the past
behind? Does some truth of common value
lie beneath the faded ink, or is it acclaim,
validation that I seek?

(cont.)

The tall scientist
and I shake hands and part, he to his task of
keeping us warm and mobile, and I to secrets
helpless before my sharpened spade.

Week Two: Lunar Eclipse

In lawn chairs, beneath blankets,
jackets, and a cover of complete
darkness, we gaze upward

through clear autumn air at
galaxies careening through space.
We can name only Ursa Major's

North Star and the sweeping
cluster of the Milky Way. Earth's
shadow blocks a full moon, total

dark in a theatre of astral
splendor. Inured to street lights,
porch lights, headlights, lights

streaming through windows, we
had not known there were so many
stars in the heavens. Then, on cue,

the lower left of the moon's orb
becomes a bright sliver, growing
imperceptibly brighter, wider—

a quarter, a half, three-quarters—
till we are bathed in silvery light
obscuring all but the brightest of

the wheeling stars above us. With
no word—no moral, no wit, no sound—
we fold our chairs and go inside.

Old Journals

At three score and eleven, he thought to
purge, molt, slough off a medley of old

selves, trace some graceful arc of new
growth, but what he found was a clamor

of magpies in cottonwoods and around
roadkill carcasses. Bronze preacher boy

in his pulpit, hand extended, rising with
lofty rhetoric to lift the roof and breach

the walls of his boxy church. God-haunted
agnostic. Vacillator who regretted all

flavors he could not taste, pilgrim and self-
flagellating hermit cast as committee chairman,

dutiful son and citizen paddling furiously
against the double leaks of desire and

doubt. Trapped romantic smashing his
sturdy house. Frustrated writer, grieving

father, lover wild with joy. Diver seeking
clarity in inky depths.

Summer of Discontent

As decisive as a butterfly. Hamster
sprinting in place, determined journey

to nowhere. Pioneer, explorer, guide,
pilgrim, drifter. Knight errant. On

the move. Commitment a sealed lid,
always leaking with bump and jostle.

A creek willy nilly making its way.
Collector of rocks, shells, pictures,

pressed flowers, newspaper clippings,
trinkets from the dance. Always words,

a winding thread through all rooms,
beside all paths, floating on all waters.

He was Houdini fiddling with lock and key,
rattling chains, bubbles rising toward

some surface he could not see. A pent
volcano blasting scoria across the foothills.

Turning Away

He knew the divorce he chose
hurt him, but forgot how he felt

choked and paralyzed for months,
pros and cons weighed by the pound

until beneath their balanced crush
he could not move. Every advance

canceled by retreat, inching forward
like a cosmic sloth, tectonic shift across

centuries. Ponderous mood swings,
Lady Fortune's wheel at high joy

already grinding toward regret and doubt.
Gazing at the lake's reflective surface,

sketching the face. An LP record hung
in the same scratchy groove till the needle

lurches sideways to a whole new song.

Eros

Love is a flood we catch
as we can. We bathe friends
in it, parents, children, sweethearts
naked in bed, splash it on dogs that
lick our hands, douse colleagues at work,
neighbors, people on our pew at church,
spray redbirds, mountain pines, blue sky,
stars at night, soak strawberries and poems
that swell with longing.

                        In it we swim, dive
to lung-bursting depths, exulting
in weightless dance. On it we launch ships
and float our bottled words. With it
we slake deepest thirst.

                        Without it,
Earth shrivels to dry sand, our body
is a valley of bones, all beauty mere
sticks, and every day is exile.

We always pray for wet—buds, blossoms,
breasts, showers, overflowing tubs, kisses,
hugs, puddles, drinks, laughter, kind deeds,
comfort, trust, hope, and, if we are lucky,
full tide under a beaming sun.

Forbidding Mourning

Our calls that fall were frequent, only
across town but over a large chasm
of guilt and uncertainty, desperate tether
to a joy so new we couldn't know it
would last. Absence measured in minutes,
hours, threatening to explode into miles
too far to travel.

Four decades later, we are half a continent
apart, our clocks on different hours, for
a month, but your calls to the house phone
outside my door are calm, details of our
common life washing over us in quiet relief:
your mom came for lunch, you paid the plumber
and cleaning lady, the dog got out, our daughter
did church with you, you got your hair cut,
you miss me, you'll be in Natchez next week.
My exotic retreat merging seamlessly:
I walked the foothills today, saw deer, hawks,
and magpie, ate frozen pasta as you suggested,
worked hours from old journals, went with
the group to a rodeo, had beers at the Mint Bar,
can't wait to see you in Denver.

No need to weep or worry. Once hot as a
welder's arc, now tempered to all weathers.

Week Three

Louder now, bolder, first names everywhere,
serving up soups, enchiladas, shish kabobs
for all. Not afraid to flip an onion. Talking

funny brother, parents, paging through
catalogues; scattered across chairs, sofas
before the wood-stove fire. "Focus! Focus!

Focus!" Blobjectivism everywhere, lazy
corners on an inflated base, without
a clue. They load up for bronc riding, blue-

grass, beers at the Mint Bar, they plan for
hot springs, attend a dirt and weed show
at a less fortunate residency. Raucous

laughter over made-up words. Friends don't
let friends bananalone. Edges smoothing,
backs relaxing, cozy beneath tin-top rain.

Still, slipping away to secret studios. Beneath
the splashing fun, sober undercurrent: which
slides, which words will they present?

Sunrise, Sunset

Like voles, they burrow
in their studios, digging

in secret, tossing up dark matter
to the light.

A Small Voice

Wearing an orange vest instead of
camel's hair or a mantle—so they can
find him on this thousand acres and so
he won't get shot—he heads into the foothills,
his new hiking boots trailing puffs of dust
behind him. It's eighteen weeks after
Pentecost, two months from Advent, and
and a whole winter, with snow gripping the hills,
before Lent. He has thirty days, not forty,
for his work. Still, it is a wilderness, and
he's alert to demons as he climbs through
brittle sage and cheatgrass going to seed.

A shy flicker lights on the ridge above him,
and magpies fuss in gulch thickets. He doubts
these birds will feed him, but hunger is no
temptation; he has frozen dinners, fruit,
sandwiches, soup, nuts, dark chocolate in
the residence house. Nor does he fear wild
beasts—black Angus cows that eye him warily
and mule deer bolting from a clump of alders.
He hopes the stiff staff he plops down at every step
will warn him of bull snakes and prairie rattlers.

Kingdoms of the earth seem remote from
these parched hills and the green alfalfa fields
in the valley below where wild turkey
forage placidly. Power in any case does
not tempt him; who would want to carry
a city or nation on his back when he can
escape scott free to an artist residency
for a month? Nor is pride of place among
his weaknesses. If he jumped from the scoria
jutting from the peak's brow, his bones
would break beside the whitened cattle skull
and ribs he sees far below.

                                        He's out for words—
a cracked door admitting light, a valve draining

stagnant cisterns, balm on chronic wounds, shade
against the simmering heat, like sturdy cottonwoods
beside a dry streambed; words that flush, like
an exploding covey of sage grouse, things he
did not know he knew, words that shape and clarify
like the stark outline of a Russian olive tree, words
that feed and those that hunt like silent hawks
with outstretched wings over grassy slopes
and washed out gulches.

                        On the tallest peak
a dry wind blows his Tilley hat, but there's no
thunder, no earthquake, no fire, thank goodness,
and as yet no still small voice from the prickly
cactus he stops beside. But as the yellowed
journals he's been reading make all too clear,
he swims in a cauldron of doubt, desire,
love, hope, guilt, fragmented intentions—
a deep pool devoid of air in its depths.

When his ancient flip-phone rings, he hears the
pained voice of his friend on a sad birthday—
the first since his wife of fifty years died. Grief
and guilt drain his friend's power, every road
is too steep. He cannot move. What to say?
That he understands? That his friend's wife
would not want him thus, that she knew his faults
and loved him still? That she is with God?
That he prays his friend joy in remembering her
and peace in giving her rest at the end? That
we live in seamless wonder beyond all our
clutching and clinging words?

                            Coming down
the sun-scorched hill on switchback cow trails,
he is chastened. He won't, like the prophet,
crown a king; his face, daubed with sunscreen,
won't shine; he won't call down fire on unrepentant
cohorts. He has paper, not stone tablets. But
he does bring words—some sharp like a scalpel,

slicing thin enough for a microscope slide, others
weak as a flashlight beam in a dusty attic, a few
rare ones packed with laughter and healing for a
wounded spirit.

                His step is firm beside the creek's
rushing current where tubing in brisk morning air
is as bracing as a baptism. Peeling off the orange vest
in the foyer of the residence house—where evening
food, friends, beer, spirited talk, and word games
await him—he heads for the familiar desk
in the Sunrise Studio, to see what he can say.

Deus Absconditis
   the hidden God

He remembers his panic at fourteen
when God moved out, vanished like

a deadbeat dad on the run, leaving
an empty sky. Alarmed, he announced God

waited for us all—then wept in the dark.
No place to hide behind a pulpit.

He was a desert guide craving water,
a pilot careening down the runway,

praying for wings, hyperventilating,
his journal a bag for breathing.

Others said they saw God at every turn,
and he imagined Him in stories

of long ago and far away, in spring
buds and flowers. Sometimes he glimpsed

His face in crowds, or felt His watching eyes
as one feels loved ones back from the dead.

As garden sank to desert, he logged the facts
and numbers, charting logic in the sand.

Hope was a hound looking for proof.
In age, he's grown an arid mind, content

with hymns, purple sweetgum leaves in fall,
the unfailing stars, friends, bread and wine,

the quiet dark before dawn.

Prayer (I)

With pre-dawn rain drumming the tin roof
of the residence house, he shuffles to the
bathroom and back. The house sleeps silently.
Supine beneath warm duvet, he counts how
rich he is—shelter from wet and cold; health,
strength despite seventy years; coffee, berries,
cantaloupe waiting in the kitchen; new friends
sleeping in nearby rooms, old friends who would
come now across all the miles if he called;
dead parents, grandparents, teachers who held
his hand, spoke him care in all of childhood;
a church that has sheltered and shaped faith
for centuries; safety, no fear his house will be
blown up; retirement income beyond all his
farm-boy dreams; poems, work in the studio
he can't wait to get to; the wife who has loved him
with passion and loyalty for four decades and
will hug him tight, kiss him in the Denver airport
a week hence; his children and children's children,
treasures beyond counting.

                                  To the divinity that
shapes and guides the curving earth, he gives thanks,
marveling at his road from childhood cotton fields
to this green and growing valley.

Sacred Space

Beyond the driveway threading north
between scoria-rock pillars; beyond
the bouncy county road where hawks
sit like sentinels on fence posts; beyond
collector Shirley's chaotic highway hillside
where broken campers, rusty trucks and
tractors, goats, horses, mules, and wandering
dogs and cats mark her home,

                              I sit in church
with denim-clad strangers, the dark-beamed
ceiling a familiar ship's hull, a nave,
stained glass windows all around telling
the old stories of love and sacrifice.

From a pew near the back, I ponder
the still, stable center of the cross above
the altar, where Being pierces Time, Word
becomes flesh. Gratitude, joy rise through
bone and breath—exhaled in wonder, praise,
astonishment that billions of crawling years
might yield this spacious moment.

                              How grew
the gestalt of swarming atoms for my body?
What first gave words to the grasping
upright form, to know and name its world?
In all the savage struggle, who knew dying
was the way to live, a soft answer bending
anger to its touch, power yielding to a tougher,
gentler force?

                        Amazed, I kneel with hands
extended for a piece of bread, a sip of wine:
common bond with people I do not know.
In phrases shaped through centuries I celebrate
what I cannot name— imagining other voices
around the teeming globe, chanting the mystery
in a medley of tongues.

(cont.)

On the highway to my home
away from home—to the studio I now
wear like a comfortable coat—the car hums,
antelopes feast in green fields, the rolling
foothills sing, and snow-capped mountains
to the west fling off their capes and dance
to the cosmic chorus.

If God were gravity

He would hold us
to the spinning earth
hurtling around the sun,
as a jolly uncle swings a child
till it's drunk with laughter.

He would balance
outstretched birds
on rising winds, planes
on their roaring upthrust,
and bright balloons adrift
on air.

He would shape the church's
soaring steeple, spruce and hemlock
like arrows, the rounded crown
of willow oaks, the upright
human form.

Instigator of all falls, he
would pull down floating feathers,
leaves in autumn, raindrops, waterfalls,
windfall apples, old buildings,
muddy hillsides, lava flowing
toward Pompeii, meteorites flaming
down the night sky, suicides
plummeting to gory death.

If God were gravity
he would dwell unseen
in every center, drawing all
to himself, inexorable as
an ocean tide, shaping with
subtle and unchanging force
the child who rises up
and every tree mouldering
on the forest floor.

Week Four: Winding Down at the Occidental

On day twenty-three of twenty-eight, they
have a modest fling at a hotel bar as old as

Custer's last stand. Beneath mounted moose
and bison heads, with guitar, piano, violin,

and horn merging behind them, and Patsy
Cline and Hank Williams bending to local

voices, they surround a table they have
seized, talking, sipping dark beer, bumping

knees. They are New York City urban and
Deep South rural, seventy-one and thirty-

three, Midwestern and Western, vegetarian
and carnivores wrestling Angus burgers big

as dinner plates. Already their minds race
toward home, where spouses, children, jobs,

pets await them. An easy comfort with
one another, rooted in their weeks together

and strengthened by the beers, hangs in
counterpoise to half-nervous smiles, an

uncertainty about what it means to pull
apart. There's good will, warmth, incipient

friendship, gratitude for the time they've had,
and something more they scarcely name:

a shared inkling that the joy of making
something new—from wood, stone, sticks,

tumbleweeds, words—is a gift to them and
somehow to their world. In the crowded

(cont.)

room couples, friends talk, neighbors for years,
and the music plays on, no one denied who

has a song. On the drive home, they speak
quietly as mule deer mill about and cross

the gravel road, unsure of these night travelers,
the deer's eyes gleaming in the car's bright beams.

The Valley of Shadow

In pastoral Piney Valley, a creek
winds along the unpaved county road,
around alfalfa fields. Cows just down from

foothill summer grazing low for their calves,
yearlings, choice steaks. A porcupine lies
unmoving in a ditch, bowled over by a car,

its bristling quills tinged with yellow. A gray
cat sits beneath a spruce, eyes locked on
a squeaking chipmunk in the tree. Nearby,

a chipmunk's collapsed carcass lingers, like
a small fur hat, on dead needles and mulch.
Beneath a twisted box elder in the hills,

a rabbit hides, still as sculpted stone, his eye
red in the picture I snap. Outside the bathroom
window, inexplicably, a kingfisher stiffens

belly-up on the gravel. Inside every door,
yellow jackets, houseflies, beetles flee
autumn's chill, sluggish, bumbling, scattered

dead on foyer floors. At a foothill crossroads,
disjointed cattle bones bleach in afternoon sun—
ribs, femur, skull. A Russian olive tree stands

stark, leafless, a mass of tangled thorns encasing
an abandoned magpie nest. A hunter's gun
booms in distant hills. Wary bucks watch

from a skyline crest, bounding with frightened
does toward protective trees.

Prayer (II)

Under a roof-battering rain in the dark, he thinks
of human need in all the bent world: of Sarah,
his paraplegic friend whose cancer bounced
from breast to liver to hip; of Jenny, the bipolar
girl locked in love and anger at the father who
shot himself a year ago. He thinks of refugees
from Syria fleeing blown up houses, dead fathers
and brothers, children cramped and hungry
in strange rooms. He remembers the mother
who leapt to cheer her son's football move
and choked to death on a piece of hard candy.

He thinks of those who have no food, no roof,
no bed, no friend to listen, say them hope;
of his brother who died a year ago not knowing
who he was, and of the friend of fifty years
whose probing words shriveled and fell silent
before the man died. He thinks of a son who
travels ruts so deep he cannot change his course,
of those trapped in their own craving for meth,
heroin, pills to erase the pain, of those driven
by hate to maim and kill others because some
voice tells them to.   He does not know how
God endures the pain. When the switchboard
lights come on and the whole grid is pulsing red,
which one does He answer? When the mother
pleads for the hungry child and there's no rice
anywhere, when microbes invade a village
and old and young die with convulsing bowels,
when earthquakes collapse houses and towns
and tsunamis toss people like twigs and drown
thousands, when fathers watch their daughters
raped and their sons' heads cut off like a piece
of firewood that's too long,

                    does He see nuances
across centuries, the circling course of every electron,
the way every atom ripples to time's quiet end, or
does He scream, weep, claw his face, kick and

fling galaxies across cosmic chasms at these
wild and swarming cries.

     ***

         With no idea how
his words might change anything save himself,
he lifts them into the cold northwestern night.

Fear No Evil

If, even in paradise, we love well what
we must leave, shall we not treasure

grass that withers, creeks draining toward
distant deserts, friends we must part with,

words that grip, like grainy photos, what's left
of one we love? Shall joy not thrive around

the woodstove for all the coming cold?

Departure

If the elusive and hungry spirit
breathes the world it's given, shapes
itself in bursts and lazy yawns, and

stretches to every corner and crevice,
will they go home broad as the high
plains sky on a clear night? Will they

shine icy bright above a darkened
moon? Will they stand tall as the steep
hill beyond the creek or the cottonwood

beside their studios? How will they
fold themselves into Vibe and Volvo,
Forester, Highlander, Prius, and Mazda

microvan to drive the long miles back
to the world they left last month? How will
spouse and child and neighbor know them?

Will they be secret and inscrutable like
rattlers gone underground in borrowed
holes on foothill slopes? Will they sit

with the alert stillness of a rabbit beneath
a box elder? Or bound away with the grace
of a mule deer clearing a five-strand fence?

Will their voice have the lilt of new friends,
the pith and wit of their talk—the warmth
of a woodstove on a cool evening? Or will

they just be annoyed at the world of clocks
and commerce, outraged at all demands,
moving with the studied arrogance of

turkeys crossing the highway before
stopped cars? Will they bristle like
the porcupine, hang taut and barbed as

(cont.)

the strands of wire no one crawls over,
taunting and fussy like distant magpies?
Will their eyes blaze with the clashing colors

of abstract art? And will the creek's cold current
bear them up in hot uncertain moments?

Legacy

And what of himself will he leave?
A shred of denim on a wild licorice bur

beside some trail. Banked ashes
in a woodstove. A whiff of bacon

in the kitchen. Cow trails infinitesimally
deeper beneath his steps in the foothills.

A slight indentation in a mattress
to shape some poet's sleep. A song that

charmed skittish cattle on a hillside path.
Ducks' wings beating the cool air above

Piney Creek. Nighttime laughter rippling
across the valley. Prayers exhaled into

the night air. Sweat stains on an orange vest.
Bicycle tracks on a gravel road. Thoughts,

twinges, thrills, inklings, dreams settling
like a lake on gulch, hill, road, creek,

and plush pasture, dormant till stirred
by some traveler lost in his own journey.

Harry Moore grew up in East Central Alabama after World War II. With degrees in English from Auburn University, Rice University, and Middle Tennessee State University, he taught freshman comp and sophomore literature in community college for four decades before retiring in 2009. His poems have appeared in *South Carolina Review, Sow's Ear Poetry Review, POEM, Penwood Review, Teaching English in the Two-Year College, English Journal, Alabama Literary Review, Avocet, The Cape Rock, Anglican Theological Review*, and other journals.

He is the author of two chapbooks: *What He Would Call Them* (Finishing Line Press, 2013) and *Time's Fool: Love Poems* (Mule on a Ferris Wheel Press, 2014).

In 2014, he received the Maureen Egen Writers Exchange Award from Poets & Writers, with a week in New York and four weeks at Jentel Artist Residency in Northeast Wyoming. Readings include the Calhoun Writers' Conference in 2013, McNally Jackson Books in Soho in 2014, the Alabama Book Festival in 2015, and the Louisville Conference on American Literature in 2016.

An assistant editor of POEM magazine, he lives with his wife, Cassandra, in Decatur, Alabama.

www.ingramcontent.com/pod-product-compliance
Lightning Source LLC
LaVergne TN
LVHW040116080426
835507LV00041B/1131